Sharpen Your Writing Skills

SHARPEN YOUR
Report
Writing Skills

Jennifer Rozines Roy

Enslow Publishers, Inc.
40 Industrial Road
Box 398
Berkeley Heights, NJ 07922
USA
http://www.enslow.com

Original edition published as *You Can Write A Report* in 2003.

Library of Congress Cataloging-in-Publication Data

Roy, Jennifer Rozines. 1967–
    Sharpen Your Report Writing Skills / Jennifer Rozines Roy.
      p. cm. — (Sharpen your writing skills)
      Summary: "Learn what goes into a report, the correct order for your information, and the final touches that make your report look amazing"—Provided by publisher.
      ISBN 978-0-7660-3905-6
      1. Report writing—Juvenile literature. I. Title.
      LB1047.3.R693 2011
      371.3'0281—dc22
      2010053476

Paperback ISBN: 978-1-59845-338-6

Printed in China

052011 Leo Paper Group, Heshan City, Guangdong, China

10 9 8 7 6 5 4 3 2 1

To Our Readers: We have done our best to make sure all Internet addresses in this book were active and appropriate when we went to press. However, the author and the publisher have no control over and assume no liability for the material available on those Internet sites or on other Web sites they may link to. Any comments or suggestions can be sent by e-mail to comments@enslow.com or to the address on the back cover.

Illustration Credits: Enslow Publishers, Inc.

Cover Illustration: Shutterstock.com

Table of Contents

Chapter One

You Can Write a Report

You sit at your desk staring at a blank piece of paper. Ever since your teacher gave you the assignment to write a report, you have procrastinated, worried, and complained. But you have not written a word. The deadline is looming, and you are starting to feel a panic attack coming on. *How will you hand in your paper by the due date if you cannot even get started?*

There is something about writing reports that makes some students nervous. They may think it is too difficult or confusing or even boring. It is true that report writing takes time and effort. But believe it or not, it can be enjoyable and exciting too.

At first I thought teachers assigned reports to drive us crazy! But now I know that learning to write them is really important!

Maybe this is your first time writing a report, and you have not really been taught how to do it. Or perhaps you have had a lousy experience in the past and want to make it better this time. Well, this book can help. It will give you the tools to write a successful report, taking you step-by-step through the research and writing processes. By the time you are finished, you will have the knowledge, the skills, and the confidence to write a terrific report. The good news is, you just may have fun along the way.

Why Do You Need to Know How to Write a Report?

First of all, it is important for school. You will probably have to do reports for many of your classes. Doing a good job may mean getting good grades and passing the class. But even after you graduate, you still may have to write reports for your job. Businesspeople, engineers, doctors, scientists, teachers, psychologists, and journalists are just some of the people who use research and report writing skills for their careers.

The rewards of writing a good report, however, are more than just a grade or paycheck. Learning about something that interests you, working hard and completing a project, and sharing the results with others will give you pride and satisfaction.

What Is a Report?

A report is a gathering of information about a subject. It tells people facts and details and presents its findings in an interesting way. A good report is based

Point of view:

When you write a report, use a third-person point of view. This point of view gives information without the writer getting personally involved in it. Do not use the words "I" or "me" or "my." Those express the first-person point of view and do not belong in a report.

First person. I think the sinking of the *Titanic* was a tragedy. I saw a movie about it, and couldn't believe it was a true story.

Third person. The sinking of the *Titanic* was a tragedy. It occurred in 1912, while the ship was crossing the Atlantic.

ZZZ . . . Wake me up when a boring report is over!

on solid research. In a report, you should try to stick mainly to the facts. Facts can be proven. They make a report accurate and strong.

Sometimes it is appropriate to include your own feelings or opinions in a report. For example, you may be writing your report to support an opinion you have. Perhaps you think that too much homework is bad for kids. In your report, you would have to find research to back that up. But however you feel about your subject, it is important to present your report in a matter-of-fact manner, using the third-person point of view.

A good report is well organized, presenting the information in an order that makes it easy to understand. A report should also be well written. When writing your report, try to use words and sentences

Make writing more fun:

Write about things that interest you. If you think your topic (what your report is about) is exciting, you will enjoy researching and writing a lot more. Even if your topic is assigned, such as "America in the nineteenth Century," your teacher may let you choose an aspect that appeals to you—pioneer children, for example, or a slave's daring escape to freedom.

Make it splash! Except for illustrations, you may need to stick with black ink on white paper for your final report. But if you're the only one who will see your research notes or rough draft, why not go nuts? Funky note paper, different colored inks . . . whatever!

Take a breather. Stressed out? Stuck? Try a five-minute jog, dance around to your favorite song, or just close your eyes and clear your mind. You'll come back to work refreshed and ready to go.

Work in a group. Unless your friends will distract you, get together and cheer each other on.

Plan something special for when your report is done. Ice cream? A movie? A long nap? Then sharpen your pencil, turn on your computer, and get to it. The sooner you start, the sooner you'll get your special treat!

that make it clear and interesting. An effective report tells the reader about something *and* keeps his or her attention from beginning to end. You do not want your audience dozing off during your report.

Finally, when all the planning, researching, and writing is complete, a report is presented to others. It might be typed on paper and read by your teacher or boss or community. It could be read aloud to your class as an oral report. However the results are shared, the last step of the report writing process is to let other people know what you have found out. This is the moment all of your hard work gets recognized, and you can pat yourself on the back and say, "I did it! I wrote a great report!"

Chapter Two

Reports—What's in Them

People write reports for different reasons. Before you write your report, think about its purpose. This will help you decide which type to write. Do you want to share information about something you have learned? Have you performed an experiment and need to present the results? Did you read a book and want to tell others about it? Or do you want to report on events that just happened?

There are different types of reports for all these different purposes. The type of report you write—and the words you use in it—can also depend on your audience. Who will be reading or listening to your report? A teacher who assigns a written science report may require a lab report with detailed results and scientific vocabulary.

However, if you are presenting a book report aloud to your classmates, you will probably use a more informal tone and express your opinion in your own words.

Research Report

A research report is the most common type of report students have to do for school. Research reports take information from different places (called sources) and present it in an organized paper. Research reports mostly discuss facts and thoughts that other people have written about.

For example, if you want to know about Martin Luther King, Jr., or the history of snowboarding, you would look up information about your subject. You might use library books, newspaper and magazine articles, and the Internet. (Find out from your teacher what kinds of sources are acceptable for the assignment.) Then you would write your report based on what you found from the various sources.

Hey, can I help?

First you do the research. Then you report it. Research report . . . get it?

Investigative Report

Another type of research report investigates and tests a problem or question. It might include research using published sources, but it also adds one important thing—your own original research. For this kind of report, you will have to collect data or conduct an experiment and present the findings. For example, let's say you want to know how many students in your school have tried smoking cigarettes. First you could research student smoking in books and magazines and on the Internet. That would give you the review of literature to write up. Then you could do a survey of your classmates. That would give you the firsthand information to answer your original question.

Lab Report

If you have a scientific question, you may want to conduct an experiment. Perhaps you are curious about how different conditions affect plant growth. Or you want to know which skin cleanser clears up acne best. Sure, you could find out what others have discovered in similar research in the past. That would be good for the section that discusses information you have found in research sources. However, doing your own experiment gives you the chance to test your ideas and prove the results. So you would perform the experiment, write up your findings, and share them in your lab report. Just make sure you follow all safety procedures for the experiment and get an adult's permission first.

Book Report

A book report is another type of report that teachers assign. A book report discusses a book that you have read. It is different from a research report, because it gives you the opportunity to give your opinion along with facts. A book report tells what the book is about and may include background information about the subject of the book and the book's author. You may choose a book you really enjoyed, one that you feel is important, or even one that you did not like at all. After you describe it, you can tell whether you recommend it or not—and why.

News Report

There is a type of report you may see every day on television or read in the newspaper. News reports inform an audience about events that are going on in

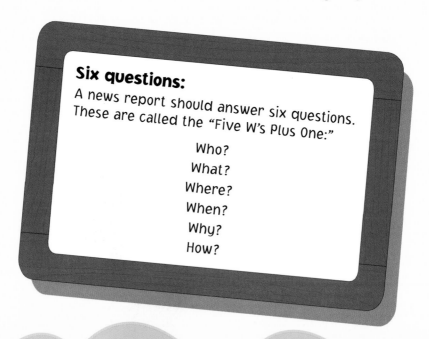

Six questions:

A news report should answer six questions. These are called the "Five W's Plus One:"

Who?

What?

Where?

When?

Why?

How?

the world. To write a news report, you gather up-to-date facts and present them to readers or listeners.

These are just some of the different types of reports students learn to write. Whether you have to do a research report, a news report, or a book report, your job as a writer is to make it clear, informative, and interesting. You may find one particular type of report easier or more enjoyable, but chances are you will have to write at least one of each type sometime in your life.

They all sound fun. I think I'll write one of each!

Types of Reports:
1. Research report
2. Investigative report
3. Lab report
4. Book report

The Parts of a Report

All reports have at least three basic parts—an introduction, a body, and a conclusion. A research report must also show where that research came from. A list of sources usually goes at the end of the report. Sources of specific facts, quotes, and ideas are also identified within the report itself. You will learn how to do these steps later in the book.

Introduction

The introduction is a paragraph that starts the report. It introduces the topic, which is the subject you are writing about. The introduction also gives a statement, called a thesis statement, that tells the main idea of your paper.

The introduction is written in a way that makes the audience want to know more. A good introduction grabs the audience's attention and sets the stage for more interesting things to come. For example, read the following introductions. Which one does a better job of getting your attention and making you want to read more?

#1—"Leeches are skinny, segmented worms. They have disks that inhale blood. Used by old-fashioned doctors for hundreds of years to remove toxins from the body, leeches are now making a comeback in modern medicine."

#2—"They are skinny. They are slimy. They are bloodthirsty creatures who have no faces. This may sound like something from a horror movie, but it is actually a description of a small animal that has helped doctors for hundreds of years. Leeches are segmented worms with sucking disks that, when used properly, can remove toxins from the human body. Long considered old-fashioned and unnecessary, leeches are now making a comeback in modern medicine."

Introduction #2 is the better choice. It instantly draws the reader in with its more interesting choice of words.

Body

The body is the middle section of the report. The body includes a number of paragraphs that present the information and findings. Every paragraph in the body is about the main topic, but each one explains a different point.

The introduction answers the questions:
"What will this report be about?"
"What is my purpose for writing it?"
"What will I be trying to explain, answer, or prove?"

The body answers the questions:
"What facts and details do I need to share?"
"How can I prove that my ideas are correct?"
"What are my results—what did I find out?"

The conclusion answers the questions:
"What was my main idea or statement?"
"Did I explain the subject, answer the question, or prove the argument?"
"Is there one point I really want people to remember?"

Conclusion

The conclusion is the paragraph that wraps everything up. A strong conclusion makes the audience feel satisfied that the writer presented a complete and effective report. The conclusion may state the main idea one last time, give a summary of the most important points, and give some last thoughts about the topic.

List of Sources

A research report includes an alphabetical list of sources at the end, usually appearing on its own page. It tells which books, magazines, newspaper articles, Web sites, or other sources you used for information about your topic.

There are two main approaches to doing this kind of list. Typically, a bibliography includes all of the sources you consulted, even if you did not end up using information from all of them. A list of works cited includes only those sources you actually took information from. Be careful, though—some people use these words differently. Make sure you know which approach your teacher prefers. Either way, however, there are specific ways of preparing the list. This will be covered later in the book.

Why is such a list required? It shows that you used enough different sources for your research. It shows that the sources you chose are appropriate and reliable. It also gives enough information that if someone else wanted to look up more stuff about your topic, they could find the sources you used. Finally, it gives credit where credit is due. When ideas or information comes from someone else's work, it is important to give them proper credit for it.

Can you say the word "bibliography" ten times fast?

Chapter Three

Getting Started

So now you know all about the different kinds of reports and what they contain. It must be time to sit down and write one, right? Not so fast! There are some things you must do before you write. This is called the *prewriting stage*. Remember, the prewriting planning you do now will make it much easier to write your report later.

The prewriting process includes choosing a topic, doing research, taking notes, writing a thesis statement, and creating an outline. This chapter and the next will take you through all of these prewriting steps, beginning with the question *"What is your report about?"* With all the many things to write about, how do you decide on a topic?

Choosing a Topic

The topic is the main subject of a report.

Sometimes a teacher will assign the topic for you. While in this case you do not have the choice about *what* to write, you still get to make your report as interesting as you possibly can. Many times, however, you will be responsible for choosing your own topic. There are steps you can take to make sure the topic you select is just right for your report.

First, decide on a general subject area. Make sure the subject interests you and is appropriate for the class.

Now focus your topic. If it is too general, there will be too much information to pack into one report.

Hot topics:
- ✔ The environment
- ✔ Current events affecting your community or school
- ✔ Health concerns
- ✔ Scientific breakthroughs
- ✔ Famous people
- ✔ Issues that affect teens
- ✔ Books by minorities and women
- ✔ Unusual hobbies or activities
- ✔ Historical events told from a unique perspective

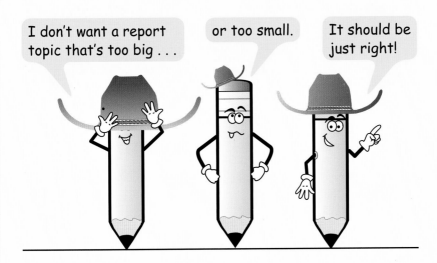

If the topic is too narrow or specific, there will not be enough information for a complete report. Do a preliminary search on your topic by skimming reference books or the Internet. This will help you see how much information is available. Once you are satisfied with your choice, check in with your teacher to make sure it is acceptable and fits the assignment.

If you are having some trouble coming up with a topic, you may try a "topic cluster." This is a graphic organizer that lets you map out your thoughts, placing a general topic in the center and brainstorming specific ideas for the branches. Once the cluster is drawn, you will have a better idea of what idea interests you *and* has the right amount of information for your report.

Temporary Thesis Statement

After you have selected your topic, you need to develop a temporary thesis statement. A thesis statement is

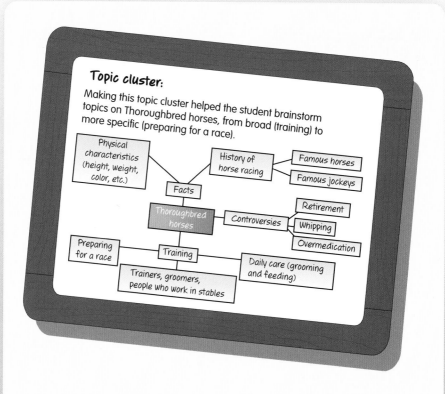

Topic cluster:
Making this topic cluster helped the student brainstorm topics on Thoroughbred horses, from broad (training) to more specific (preparing for a race).

one sentence that tells the main point or argument you will make in your paper.

"But how am I supposed to know what my main point is when I have not done my research?" you may ask. The answer: You're not. That's where the word *temporary* comes in. Nothing is final here. At this point, you are just making a guess about what you *think* you will discover or prove. You may change your temporary thesis statement at any time during your research. For now, however, it gives you a good starting point and sets you off in the right direction for your research.

The Research

There are many, many places to find facts and details about your topic. These places are called reference sources. Primary reference sources are eyewitness accounts or original documents. Letters, diaries, and personal interviews are primary sources. Secondary sources take their information from somewhere else. Magazines, books, and Internet articles are examples of secondary sources.

It is up to you to decide which sources offer you the best research information. To help you evaluate your source, ask yourself the following three questions.

Examples of temporary thesis statements:

✔ Some practices used in training Thoroughbred racehorses are inhumane and should be abolished.

✔ Soap and water are more effective in treating adolescent acne than expensive skin cleansers.

✔ Jane Austen was an important writer who captured the social attitudes of her era.

If you can answer "yes" to all of them, you will know you have found a good source for your report.

1. Is this information useful? You cannot include everything you find in every book or article about your topic. Only use information that gives you facts, details, and opinions that relate directly to your report. Your goal is to support (or contradict) your thesis statement— not fill pages about everything everyone has ever said about your topic.

2. Is the material up-to-date? Whenever you find a source that you plan to use, be sure to check the date that it was published. Knowledge and ideas change over time. Therefore, try to find the most recent information available. It takes a while for books to be printed and information to be kept current. Although older books and articles may be accurate, your best bet is usually to use newer published sources. One advantage of researching over the Internet is that the information can be updated more easily. Online documents and sites usually list the original date of publication, and then note newer dates if the material was revised. Look over these dates to determine whether the online information is current or outdated.

3. Is the source reliable? This is important. Not all sources are accurate or trustworthy. Sometimes the person who wrote the information you

have found has certain beliefs or prejudices about the topic. An author who uses emotional language, presents only one side of an issue, or makes unproven or inaccurate statements will not give you solid research. Of course, many writers have an opinion about their subject. It is when their opinions get in the way of the accuracy or believability of their writing that the source becomes unreliable.

How do you evaluate a source for reliability? After all, you are a student doing a report—not an expert. A good way to evaluate a resource is by checking the sources the author used. Look over the list of works cited. A good list has titles that are reputable, balanced, and up-to-date. Something else you can do is use books by well-known publishers and articles from magazines with good reputations. Another helpful method is to look up the author's background. Does the author have the education, expertise, or experience to write knowledgeably about the topic? Perhaps you could even find some reviews of the source and see what other experts think about this author and his or her writing.

Internet Sources

Be extra careful about using information from the Internet. It is safest to use sites published by respected organizations (.org), educational institutions (.edu), and government agencies (.gov). You may decide to use material from a Web site with the suffix .com, but first make sure you know about the source to be sure it is truthful. (Sites with the suffix .com are usually for-profit companies, so they may be trying to sell you something.)

Finding Sources

Where do you find reference sources? The best place to begin your research adventure is the library. The library's reference section contains books, articles, directories, microfilms, and videos. If you are unfamiliar with the reference section or have a question during your research, ask a librarian for help.

Before you begin your search, it is useful to have a few keywords written down. A keyword is a word or phrase related to your topic. (For instance, the student doing the report on Thoroughbred racing might have the keywords "Thoroughbred," "horse racing," and "jockey.")

Your keywords can help you find printed material in the library in several ways:

- Type your keywords into the library's computer catalog to find books on your topic.

- Use your keywords to search INFOTRAC, which allows you to look online for magazines and newspaper articles.

- Look in print reference works such as encyclopedias using your keywords. (Some teachers don't allow students to use encyclopedias, so be sure to check with your teacher first.)

- Look in the *Reader's Guide to Periodical Literature* to locate magazine articles.

The key is to find some keywords. They will unlock the doors to your research!

Again, your librarian can be a big help directing you to good sources you may not even know exist.

Once you find the title of a source that interests you, write it down. If it is a book, write down the call number. The call number, or Dewey decimal number, tells you where to find the book in the library. If the source is a magazine or newspaper article, write down the volume number and date it was published. Now go find the sources in the library and take a look inside to see if they have the information you need.

Searching the Net

You can also use your keywords to find material on the Internet. Many Internet providers offer search engines, such as Google, that allow you to explore their directories. The search engine will find Web sites that can help you with your report. Remember to evaluate your sources to make sure they are reliable.

Working Bibliography

A working bibliography is a list of sources you think you might use for your report. It is useful in two ways. First, it helps you keep track of your sources while you research and write. Second, it provides the information you will need for your final bibliography or list of works cited. This could save you a lot of time and possible confusion later.

Whenever you find a book or article that looks helpful, write down all of the information you would need to include it in your final bibliography or list of works cited: the title, the first and last names of the author(s), the publisher's name, and so forth. Different kinds of sources may require different kinds of information. For example, you may need to identify the volume number for an encyclopedia or magazine article, or the date you looked up an Internet article. A more complete discussion of the kind of information needed for your final list of sources, and exactly how to write it down, appears later in the book.

Finding Primary Sources

Primary sources—original documents and accounts by eyewitness—make a report interesting and unique. Sometimes it is good to talk directly to people to get firsthand information. An interview is a meeting where you ask questions and gather information. You may want to interview an expert in a particular field or a person who witnessed the event you are writing about. Contact the person by phone, mail, or e-mail. Many adults are eager to share their knowledge and will agree to help with a student's report. If your source is unavailable or deceased, check the library for diaries, speeches, letters, or taped "oral histories."

Hello, White House? I'd like to ask the president a few questions for my report. Hello? Hello?

Again, it is important to evaluate the source of your information. Just because one person tells you something, it does not necessarily make it true. Try to interview experts who are up-to-date in their knowledge, or use written sources that have been evaluated by experts. While you are putting together the working bibliography, make sure that you use a variety of sources. If you take different viewpoints into account, you will get better balanced research for a more effective report.

Another kind of primary source can be—you! In the next chapter you'll find out more about conducting your own experiments and organizing your data.

Chapter Four

Getting the Right Stuff in the Right Order

Piles of books and articles. Pages and pages of information. How can you get the facts and ideas you need for your report without spending hours reading and copying?

First of all, you are not expected to read everything word for word. Look over your source first to get an idea of the exact places that have the information you want. Check out the table of contents, index, or beginning paragraphs to help focus your search. Then skim the material for keywords or ideas that catch your eye.

Next, it is time to take notes. If you are writing notes by hand, you will need a stack of index cards. If you have a note-taking program on your computer, you can do the following steps electronically. Write one idea or fact on each card.

Super note-taking method:

```
┌─────────────────────────────────────┐
│ 1. Author              2. Keyword    │
│                                      │
│            3. Your Notes             │
│                                      │
│                                      │
│              4. Page Numbers         │
└─────────────────────────────────────┘
```

1. Write the author's name in the top left corner to keep track of the source of this information.
2. Write a word that describes what these notes are about. You can use the keyword to help you organize your notes later.
3. Include facts and ideasthat look useful.
4. Write the number of the page(s) on which the information was found.

Example:

```
┌─────────────────────────────────────┐
│ Crum                      history    │
│                                      │
│ first thoroughbred from Arabian      │
│ stallion and English mare in late    │
│ 17th century                         │
│                           42-43      │
└─────────────────────────────────────┘
```

Plagiarizing is no joke! Even a funny guy like me takes it seriously.

Remember, you absolutely must give proper credit when you use information. Copying someone else's words or ideas and pretending they are your own is called plagiarizing. Plagiarizing is illegal. It is stealing someone else's work. Plagiarizing can get you a flunking grade or even get you expelled. It is a serious matter, so be careful to use your own words and ideas or show where you got the information. Writing the source of each note on your card will help ensure that you give credit where credit is due.

The notes you take will either *paraphrase* or *quote* the information you find. To paraphrase, write down what you have read using your own words. To quote, copy the information word for word. Then, put quotation marks around the quotes. You can quote a sentence or a whole paragraph. Try not to use too many quotations in your report. You want to show plenty of original thinking and writing.

Examples:

Paraphrase: Horse owner Amy Lexus thinks that training methods are kinder to animals than they used to be.

Quote: "Current training practices are much more compassionate than they were in the past."
                                        —horse owner Amy Lexus.

If your quote is several lines long, you may need to set it off in a block quotation. To do this, begin a new line, indenting about one inch from the left margin. Even though it is a direct quote, you do not have to use quotation marks for a block quotation. It will be clear from the way it is indented.

Example of a block quotation:

> Most schoolchildren who have been bullied feel unsafe long after the bullying incident. Bullies threaten more vulnerable children with future violence, which makes the victim feel almost constant apprehension and insecurity. Although kids have always had conflicts, these days bullies are much more apt to escalate into rougher and more violent behavior.

After you have gone through all your reference sources and taken the notes you need from each, look through your cards. Do you have enough information for your report? Are there any leftover gaps or questions you have? If you answered "yes," go back to the library or computer and continue your research. If you answered "no," your research of materials is complete.

Doing Your Own Research

You have gathered information from primary and secondary sources. But what about your own research? If you need original findings—ones you discover yourself—it is time to collect some data. Doing your own research is fun, but keeping your data organized is tricky. Here's how!

Show validity and reliability. Collect your data to the best of your ability. Then you can be a good researcher, just like me!

Data is specific, factual information that can help you support your thesis statement. When you record and report your data, it is important to be careful and accurate.

The method of collecting data you choose must have validity and reliability. *Validity* means that you are really measuring what you say you are measuring. For example, suppose you are testing the amount of rainfall in your backyard. You accidentally leave the rain collector underneath a gutter that drips. The water drips get mixed in with the raindrops. Therefore, your test is not valid.

Reliability means that someone else could follow your steps exactly and get similar results. To show that your data is reliable, you should write down what you do in detail. That way, anyone could do a retest and see that your procedure was reliable.

Surveys

One method of gathering data is by doing a survey. To conduct a survey, the researcher asks a question or questions to a group of people. The survey can be done by written questionnaire or by asking face-to-face or over the phone.

Let's say you want to find out the most popular school lunch. You could survey your classmates face-to-face and write down their answers. Or you could hand out questionnaires that ask students to write in a vote for their favorite lunch along with any comments.

Experiments

Experiments are also a good way to collect data. An experiment is a controlled procedure carried out to discover, test, or demonstrate something.

When conducting an experiment, write down everything you use. These are called the materials. List the number and amounts in detail so that your materials list is very clear. Now perform your experiment. Write down everything you did, step-by-step. This is called your method. Finally, record your data. All of these notes will be very helpful when you write your report.

You may want to display your data in a table or graph. A table helps to organize your information in

Table

President's Physical Fitness Award Qualifications

Age	1-mile run (minutes:seconds)	Pull-ups
Boys		
10	7:57	6
11	7:32	6
12	7:11	7
Girls		
10	9:19	2
11	9:02	2
12	8:23	3

rows (that go across) and columns (that go down). Write a title above your chart to tell what results it shows.

Graphs are pictures of data that use bars, shapes, or lines to show results. Some types of graphs are line graphs, bar graphs, and pie graphs. Visual displays of your findings will help you see patterns and make judgments about your research.

Take a look at your results. Are they the results you expected? Sometimes an experiment will prove that your temporary thesis statement was right. Other times, it will show something else. Do not change your data even if things do not turn out the way you thought they would. The purpose of an experiment is to discover the answer to a question. No matter what the answer turns out to be, write down the results exactly.

Oops! My research showed something different than I'd thought. I'll have to change my thesis statement. Good thing I have a big eraser. . .

research check

The Final Thesis Statement

Remember back at the beginning of the prewriting stage, when you came up with a statement that you thought would sum up your report? Now that you have taken your notes and discovered results, look back at that temporary thesis statement. Do you still agree with it? If your research supports it, keep it. If the

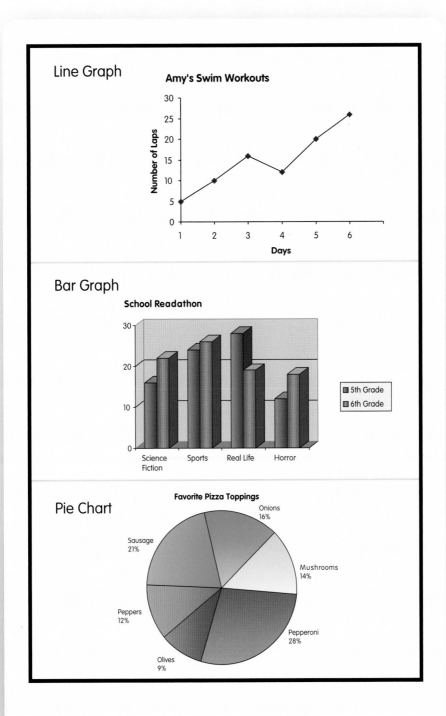

Line Graph

Amy's Swim Workouts

Bar Graph

School Readathon

- 5th Grade
- 6th Grade

Science Fiction | Sports | Real Life | Horror

Pie Chart

Favorite Pizza Toppings

Onions 16%
Sausage 21%
Mushrooms 14%
Peppers 12%
Pepperoni 28%
Olives 9%

things you have learned since you wrote it have made you change your mind, write a new thesis statement. Your thesis statement should now represent the ideas in your final report.

The Outline

An outline organizes the information you have collected. Your completed outline is the general map that will guide you to smooth report writing.

An outline shows the main ideas and supporting details and how they will be divided into paragraphs. The main ideas are written next to Roman numerals. The facts and details that support those ideas are written below them next to letters.

Begin creating your outline by looking over your note cards. Check out the keywords you wrote in the upper right corners. This will give you a reminder of the main ideas and issues you will discuss in your report.

I'm King of Note Card Mountain!

Sort Your Note Cards

The next step of the prewriting process is to organize your index cards. Sort your cards according to subject. Make a pile of each main idea. Then add the cards that contain the corresponding facts and details to each pile. Finally, make one giant stack from the individual piles, placing the main ideas and details in the best order. Now you have all the information you will be writing about in order. Handy, right?

There are different formats for outlines, depending on the number of main ideas and details. Here is one possible outline format and an example to show you what an outline can look like.

Title

    I. Introduction
        A. Opening statement
        B. Background
        C. Thesis statement

    II. Main Idea #1
        A. Supporting detail
        B. Supporting detail
        C. Supporting detail

    III. Main Idea #2
        A. Supporting detail
        B. Supporting detail
        C. Supporting detail

    IV. Main Idea #3
        A. Supporting detail
        B. Supporting detail
        C. Supporting detail

    V. Conclusion
        A. Review of major issues and ideas
        B. Results, solution, final thoughts

Example:

Controversies in Thoroughbred Racing

    I. Introduction
        A. Racing and training Thoroughbreds is big business
        B. About Thoroughbreds
        C. Some of today's practices are inhumane and should be abolished

    II. History
        A. Racing and training in the 1800s
        B. Racing and training in the 1900s

    III. Whipping
        A. Why is it done
        B. How it affects horses
        C. Healthier alternatives

    IV. Overmedicating
        A. When it happens
        B. How it affects horses
        C. Healthier alternatives

    V. Retirement
        A. "Glue factories" and abuse
        B. Different work opportunities
        C. Healthier alternatives

    VI. Conclusion
        A. Review of issues
        B. Final reminder—there are many ways to keep Thoroughbreds healthy and happy while racing and training

Congratulations on completing all of the thinking, planning, researching, and organizing that the prewriting process requires.

Chapter Five

It's Time to Write!

You are now ready to write the first draft of your report. The first draft is your first try at getting all the facts and ideas on paper. It does not have to be perfect. First drafts give the writer the chance to write without worrying about spelling, grammar, and neatness. The most important thing is to include all the facts and ideas. Feel free to make changes along the way.

Starting Up

Take the information from your outline and note cards and start writing. Use your own words as much as possible, adding exact quotes where you think they fit best. If, for example, you find a really interesting or unusual sentence or passage that relates to your thesis statement—quote it.

Example:

Theo Robins, president of Robotix, Inc., says, "Robot best friends will be the next big toy for kids in this technological age."

Your report should be written in paragraphs. A paragraph contains a group of sentences that all discuss one main idea. A well-written paragraph has one topic sentence, which states the main idea of that paragraph. The other sentences have facts and details that support or help explain the topic sentence. Begin a new paragraph each time you write about a new main idea.

Example (good paragraph, topic sentence underlined):

The latest craze in ice cream flavors is … vegetables! That's right— the icky things your mom makes you eat before you can have dessert. Broccoli, squash, spinach, and beets have been swirled into the dessert itself. Ten local stores are carrying this nutritious frozen concoction.

Example (bad paragraph, no topic sentence):

The Madagascar chameleon lives there. Some reptiles spit their own saliva out as a weapon. The homes of the desert snakes are not easily found by predators.

If you get stuck while writing your rough draft, do not get discouraged. You may need to take a break for a few minutes. But do not take too much time away from your paper, and do not give up! Keep writing.

The more you write, the easier it will get—and the closer you will be to getting your report done.

> When I get stuck, I like to stand on my head and hope the right words rush down into my brain.

✓ The Format

Different types of reports have different formats to follow.

Research Paper

Write your introduction. Include some background information and your thesis statement.

Write the body next. This section should contain the facts and details you gathered during your review of literature. If you conducted original research such as an interview, a survey, or an experiment, write it up here. List the materials you used, your method and procedures, and your findings.

Now comes the conclusion. The conclusion is the last paragraph or paragraphs in your report. This is your last chance to put your ideas and main points into your audience's mind. A good way to begin your conclusion is to restate your thesis statement. This will remind the reader or listener of the main idea of your report. Next, summarize the important points you have already discussed. Do not add any new information here. Just briefly sum up what your research has shown. Finally, give some last thoughts about your topic. Try to leave the audience satisfied that you proved your point. Wrap up your report with confidence.

The list of sources and any other additional pages (like survey forms or data charts) go at the end of your report.

Book Report

Write the introduction. Give the title and author and a few sentences that introduce the book.

In the body, give facts and details about the book. If it is fiction, tell about the characters (people) and setting (time and place). Discuss the plot (action in the story), but be sure you do not give away the ending. If the book is nonfiction, explain what kind of book it is (biography, travel, history, science, etc.). Give some information that was included in the book.

You may want to share your opinion about the book. What did you think of it? Why? Give examples to explain why you feel this way. Be specific. Describe scenes that surprised, scared, or excited you. Offer a quote by a character that made you laugh or groan. Discuss ideas or themes that made you think. Be sure to mention how the book made you feel. Did it touch your heart, motivate you to do something new, or cause you to feel sad?

After you have covered everything you want your audience to know, write your conclusion. Wrap up the main points. Tell why you would or would not encourage others to read this book.

News Report

Write the introduction with an attention-grabbing "lead." Try to make the audience interested right away.

My body contains facts and details too!

The body includes facts and details that are up-to-date. If your story is about current events, give some background about the people and places involved. For a human interest story (one about everyday people's lives), offer information that makes the audience feel as if they want to know those people. A sports report should contain scores, highlights, and details about the athletes that made the game interesting.

Your conclusion should be brief and to the point. A sentence or two that retells the main idea of the story will complete the news report.

Document Your Sources

In addition to your final bibliography or list of works cited, you will be giving credit to your reference sources throughout your paper. Each time you include specific information from another source—a fact, a quote, or another person's idea—you will identify which source and which page that information came from.

There are several ways of doing this. Some teachers prefer in-text citations, which sound difficult but are pretty easy to work with. This is the method we will concentrate on in this book. Other teachers prefer footnotes or endnotes. You have probably seen this method used in books. It involves using numbers in the text that correspond to reference notes at the bottom of the page (for footnotes) or at the end of the report (for endnotes).

For in-text citations, instead of using numbers to refer the reader elsewhere, you will actually cite (tell) the source within the report. Most of the time, this involves putting the author's last name in parentheses after the information you used, along with the page number the information actually came from:

Paul Smith, president of the Snow Club of America, says that snowboarding has become more popular every single year for the past five years. (Quinby 41)

By the way, if you are quoting directly from the source—using exactly the same words—be sure to put quotation marks around the part that is the same. That shows it is someone else's wording. If you decide to use your own words instead, make sure they are different enough that you do not seem to be copying—and that the meaning is still the same as what the author intended.

What if you are using the author's name right in the sentence? Then you only need to give the correct page number in parentheses:

Kim Muggleton, an expert on winter sports, says, "Until very recently, skiing was the most popular sport on Whiteout Mountain." (91) Now, however, Muggleton says that snowboarding "is just as popular as skiing." (93)

If there are two authors, write both of their names: (Quinby and Sidney 292). If there is no author, write the name of the source instead: (Teen Beat 85).

Revising — Making It Better

The first draft is done. You have written your ideas down in the approximate form and order you had in mind. But do not worry if it does not look or sound exactly the way you had hoped. No writer gets it right the very first time. That is why you must revise it. Revising means making changes that make your report the best it can be.

First, skim over your whole report. Does it say what you want to say? Does it make your main points? Next, look at the paragraphs. Is the information organized and placed in the right order? Does each paragraph contain one main idea? Are there facts and details missing? Is there anything that should be added or taken out? Finally, read your sentences out loud to someone else, if possible. Do the words and sentences make sense? Is your writing style clear and interesting?

This report needs a tune-up. Time to revise!

Rewrite and fix all the problem spots. Your new and improved report should have a good writing style, organized ideas, and correct facts that support your topic.

Edit and Proofread

Your next job is to check spelling, grammar, and punctuation. Now is the time to get rid of all mistakes. Use a dictionary or computer spell-checker to help with your editing. (But be careful: Spell-checkers make mistakes—often they don't recognize names, and they can't tell if a correctly spelled word is being used incorrectly.) It is also a good idea to ask another person to look over your report for errors.

Look carefully at the words. Did you spell them correctly and use them properly? Inspect the grammar. Are the parts of speech right? Are the sentences complete? Examine the punctuation. Did you use commas, periods, and quotation marks correctly? Did you use a certain word too many times? If so, find a synonym or similar word to avoid repetition. Make all the corrections needed.

The Final Draft

If you have time before your report is due, set your work aside for a day or so. This will give your mind a break, and you will be able to see the report with "fresh eyes."

When you are sure you are satisfied that your report is in good shape, write or type the final draft. (Chapter 6 will give you specific ideas of how to make it look polished.) The final draft shows off the results of all your hard work, so make it neat and mistake-free.

Bibliography, or Works Cited

At the end of your report, you will need either a bibliography (a list of all the sources you found) or a list of works cited (all the sources you actually took information from.) Ask your teacher which approach you should use. Either way, it usually goes on a separate page, with the heading "Bibliography" or "Works Cited" at the top.

Now find your working bibliography from the research stage. Check off the sources you will include in your bibliography or list of works cited. Write or type them in alphabetical order according to the author's last name. If the source does not have an author, use the first word of the title (not including *A*, *An*, or *The*).

There is a special style to use for a bibliography or list of works cited, and the information included for each source may differ depending on what type of source it is. Ask your teacher which style he or she prefers, or ask if you can follow these examples:

Book

Style: Author's Last name, First name. <u>Title</u>. City, State: Publisher, Copyright date.

Example: Smith, Joan. <u>All About Computers</u>. Chicago, Ill.: Big City Books, 2012.

Encyclopedia Article

Style: "Subject or Article Title." <u>Name of encyclopedia</u>. Volume number or edition, Date, Page numbers.

Example: "Software." <u>Encyclopedia Smith</u>. Vol. 14, 2012, pp. 183–185.

Magazine Article

Style: Author's last name, First name. "Article Title." <u>Name of magazine</u>. Volume number, Issue number, Date, Page numbers.

Example: Jackson, Vikki. "The Computer Age Cometh." <u>Computer Monthly</u>. Vol. 10, Issue 3, March, 2012, pp. 41–47, 49.

Newspaper Article

Style: Author's last name, First name. "Article Title." <u>Name of newspaper</u>. City, State. Date, Page numbers.

Example: Smitt, Samuel. "Is Your Hard Drive Driving You Crazy?" <u>The City Times</u>. Mannville, Calif. October 14, 2012, p. D1.

Internet Article

Style: Author's last name, First name. "Article Title." <u>Name of Web site</u>, date article was published or posted, Internet address (date you found article).

Example: Blakely, Carol. "Faster Downloads." <u>Blakely's Easy Guide to Downloading</u>, April 4, 2012, http://www.blakdown.com/ fstdwnld.12264 (November 3, 2012).

Now that you've put your final list together, check to make sure everything has been alphabetized, copied, and spelled correctly. Add it to your final draft.

Now you're ready for the very last step in writing your report—publishing!

Chapter Six

The Finishing Touches

The last stage of the writing process is publishing. Publishing means preparing and sharing your report. After everything you have done to write your "masterpiece," you know you want it to look as nice as possible.

Whether you are writing by hand or typing the report, there are some guidelines to follow. Unless your teacher suggests otherwise, use white, 8½-by-11-inch paper. Write on only one side of the paper. Leave one-inch margins on all sides. Number all of the pages ½ inch from the top in the upper right corner. If you are typing your report, double space.

Title Page

Some report writers like to create a title page. The title page comes at the beginning of the report. Different teachers have different rules about how to create a title page. Be sure to follow your teacher's rules. One method writers use is to type the title and center it about a third of the way down the paper. Capitalize the first letter of each important word in the title. Then go down to about two thirds of the way down and type your name, double space to the next line and put the instructor's name, then double space down one more time for the date.

Special Effects

Computers can do lots of things to enhance the presentation of a report. They offer different type styles and fonts. They help create tables, charts, and graphs for illustrations. Computers can make reports look neat, attractive, and professional. What they cannot do is hide the faults of a poorly written report. Computers cannot make bad reports good; they make good reports *look* good.

Graphics are illustrations in a report. Graphics should be used to provide important information (not just take up space). A good picture can show an example of something discussed in the report and help the reader remember it better. People often remember graphic images more than words. Maps and diagrams are examples of illustrations commonly seen in reports.

Tables, charts, and graphs present information that includes data, numbers, and statistics. Instead of reading through a lot of numbers and trying to figure out what they all mean, your readers will be able to look at graphics that show the information in a form that is easy to use and understand.

Always tell the readers what the graphics are and what they mean. What is this illustration? Why are you showing it? Give the graphic a title. Below the title, write the source where you found the information. Discuss the main points of the graphic in your report.

All right! You have researched, organized, written, revised, and edited. It took many steps to get to this point, and it is *almost* time for you to celebrate. But first you need to evaluate your report. Is it as good as

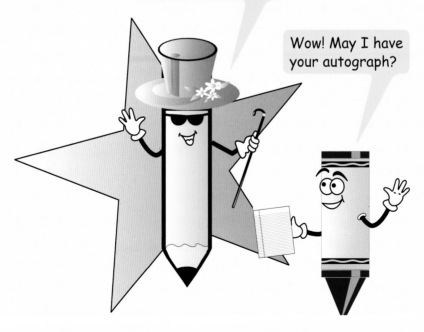

you can possibly make it? Look it over one more time and ask yourself the questions on the Final Checklist.

Final checklist:

1. Did I choose a good topic? Is it appropriate for the class or audience? Is it interesting? Was there enough information about the subject to complete the report?

2. Is the introduction interesting? Does it make you want to read more?

3. Did I prove my thesis statement?

4. Are the paragraphs organized in the best order? Does each paragraph contain one main idea?

5. Does the conclusion give a strong ending?

6. Have I edited and proofread properly?

7. Is the bibliography or works cited accurate and complete?

8. Does the published report look neat and polished?

9. Am I satisfied with my report? Is there anything I would change?

Binding the Report

Reports should be stapled, covered, or bound. There are a variety of covers available. Many teachers prefer clear plastic front covers. Professional binding, including spiral binding, can be done at office supply and copy shops. Depending on the number of people with whom you will share your report, you can make one copy or many.

Presenting ... Your Report!

One way of publishing your report is to display it. Your teacher may want to post it on a display table for your classmates to see. Sometimes teachers will show off students' work at open houses and parent conferences. Ask your teacher to exhibit your report if he or she does not suggest it first.

Another method of publishing is distribution—making copies of your report and handing them out to others.

The Internet can be an effective publishing tool. There are Web sites where you can share your work. This way, many

Wow! This is a great report!

Hot off the press! Get the latest research here!

Main Street USA

MY REPORT!

MY REPORT!

people (even some you will never meet) can benefit from your knowledge. Make sure you choose a site with a good reputation. If you have your own home page, you can publish it there.

One problem with publishing reports on the Internet is the possibility of plagiarism. Publishing online can give other students the opportunity to copy your report, or parts of your report, and turn it in under their own names. Use good judgment or ask an adult for advice if you decide to publish this way.

Oral Reports

A popular way of presenting a report is by reading it aloud in front of a group of people. This is known as an oral report. An oral report is a bit different from a written report. An oral report covers the material you have researched, but it is presented in a more conversational tone. Many teachers will not allow students to read from their reports word for word. This makes your oral report sound too stiff. Instead of reading straight from your written report, you may use your note cards to remind you what to say and in which order to say it.

To prepare for an oral report, practice beforehand to get comfortable. Learn your report well enough so that you can look up at your audience now and then. You do not want to give the entire report with your face down. After you have rehearsed your report enough that you feel confident, do a "trial run" in front of others. Ask for their suggestions on how to improve your presentation.

Standing up in front of other people can be a little scary. Before you give your oral report, take a deep breath and try to relax. Speak slowly and clearly. Remember, you did a lot of work to make your report good—you want people to hear it. Finally, remind yourself that you have interesting information to share. Your audience will be more interested in listening to your report if you are excited about it yourself.

In Conclusion …

However you decide to present your report, the important part is that you feel good about the work you put into it. Writing a report takes commitment. Publishing your report shows that you can finish what you have started. It may seem like a long time since you first found out you had to write a report. I hope this book has helped to make the steps between that moment and this one easier and more enjoyable.

Congratulations! You wrote a report!

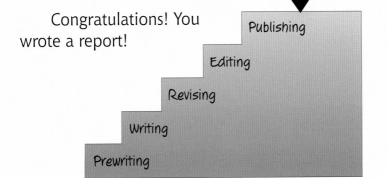

Publishing

Editing

Revising

Writing

Prewriting

A Sample Student Research Report

The Better Balloon

Amy Gregory
Science 6
July 10, 2012

Introduction

Thesis
statement

Birthdays, graduations, and anniversaries are special occasions. They are often celebrated with balloons. These days, consumers have the choice between two different kinds of balloons—latex and Mylar. While Mylar balloons are more expensive, they are a better buy because they last longer and are harder to break.

Main idea:
general
background
information;
citing
research
sources

For many years balloons were only made of latex. Latex is a gooey material that comes from plants. Chemicals are added to the plant base to make it elastic. (DeVillers 14) The elasticity makes the balloon stretch as gas is pushed into it.

In the 1980s, Mylar balloons were introduced to the public. Mylar is a man-made polyester material made of very thin sheets. (Quinby 1) It also stretches when gas enters it.

Both latex and Mylar balloons are sold in stores. At the North Mountain Gift Shop, latex balloons sell for $1.00 apiece. Mylar balloons cost $2.50 each. According to shop owner Susan Lindsley, Mylar balloons are a better buy in spite of their higher price. "Mylar balloons last longer than latex balloons. They also tend to pop less. Mylar sometimes seems unbreakable," says Lindsley.

Latex balloons and Mylar balloons differ in the way they retain helium. Helium is a colorless gas that is lighter than air. When helium is inserted and trapped in balloons, the balloons float. Eventually, the helium in any balloon will escape, and the balloon will fall to the ground. The spaces between latex molecules let tiny amounts of helium out. In Mylar, the chemical bonds between the molecules are much tighter than those in latex. A Mylar balloon holds the helium gas in better than latex. (Hamilton 7)

An experiment was conducted on both types of balloons to test their durability.

Materials:
  2 latex balloons—round, filled with helium to 12-inch diameter
  2 Mylar balloons—round, filled with helium to 12-inch diameter
  1 3-inch sharp pin

In the experiment, the pin was jabbed into one latex balloon. It popped immediately. The pin was jabbed into one Mylar balloon. The balloon was dented temporarily, then resumed its shape. It did not pop. It required twelve jabs to break the Mylar balloon. The experiment was performed again with two new balloons. This time, it took two jabs to pop

Main ideas with supporting details: Mylar is more expensive but better; citing primary sources

Topic sentence

Main idea with supporting details: The two types of balloons hold helium differently

Main idea with supporting details: Is Mylar more durable? Description of the experiment.

the latex balloon. After two jabs, the Mylar balloon still remained intact. After ten pin jabs, the Mylar balloon popped. The pin thrusts were approximately even in force, to the best of the experimenter's ability.

Graphic–
bar graph
showing
data

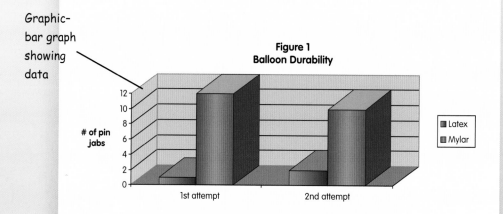

Figure 1
Balloon Durability

# of pin
jabs

Latex
Mylar

1st attempt   2nd attempt

Main
idea with
supporting
details:
Is the
experiment
reliable?

    The results of this experiment might be further verified by more accurate testing. For example, a machine could be used to puncture the balloon material, which would eliminate human error, in strength of jabs. However, the experiment did prove that Mylar balloons perform better than latex to a certain degree of reliability.

Conclusion —

Repeats
thesis
statement

    Although Mylar balloons cost more than latex, they are worth the price. They are stronger, thereby making them safer. For consumers who want balloons that do not tend to break easily, Mylar is the better choice!

Works Cited

DeVillers, Quinn. *Science Facts*. Columbus, Ohio: Readmore Books, 1996.

Hamilton, Jack. "Rubber Bubbles," *Kid Science*, July 2000:7.

Quinby, Robin. *Toy Science*. New York: Young Publishers, 2002.

Glossary

audience—The people who read or hear what you have written.

body—The writing between the introduction and conclusion that develops the main idea.

brainstorming—Gathering ideas by thinking about all of the possibilities.

data—Information (such as facts, figures, and examples) from which conclusions can be drawn.

draft—A piece of writing not in its final form.

graphic organizer—A display of ideas.

introduction—The beginning of the report.

prewriting—The planning stage before writing.

quote—To use someone else's words directly.

report—A piece of writing that results from researching and organizing facts about a topic.

revise—To change writing so that it is improved.

source—A reference for information.

thesis statement—A sentence that tells the purpose or main idea.

topic—The main idea.

works cited page—A list of the sources used in a report.

Further Reading

Books

Loewen, Nancy. *Just the Facts: Writing Your Own Research Report.* Minneapolis, Minn: Picture Window Books, 2009

Northey, Margot. *Making Sense: A Student's Guide to Research and Writing.* Don Mills, Ont.: Oxford University Press, 2005.

Terban, Marvin. *Find It! Write it! Done!: Your Fast and Fun Guide to Research Skills that Rock*! New York: Scholastic, 2007

Internet Addresses

Writing a Book Report
<http://www.webspawner.com/users/BBBookReport>

Writing-World.com
<http://www.writing-world.com>

Index

A
audience, 10, 14

B
bibliography, 18, 28, 48–50
binding, 54–55
body, 15, 16, 17
book reports, 14, 44
brainstorming, 21

C
computer effects, 52–53
conclusion, 15, 17
cover, 54–55

D
data collection, 33–36
drafts, 41–43, 47–48, 50

E
editing, 47–48
experiments, 35–36

F
final draft, 48, 50
first draft, 41–43
first person, 7
formats, 43–45

G
graphic organizers, 21
graphics, 52–53
graphs, 36, 37, 52

I
illustrations, 52–53
Internet, 24, 25–26, 27, 55–56
introduction, 15–16, 17
investigative reports, 13

L
lab reports, 13

N
news reports, 14–15, 45
note taking, 31–34

O
oral reports, 56–57
outline, 38–40

P
plagiarizing, 32, 56
presentation, 55–57
prewriting, 19, 40
primary sources, 28–29
proofreading, 47–48
publishing, 51, 55–57

Q
quotations, 32–33, 41–42

R
Reader's Guide to Periodical Literature, 27

reference sources, 12, 18, 23–29, 45–47, 48–50
reliability, 34
research process, 23–29
research reports, 12, 18, 43–44
revision, 47

S
sample report, 58–61
sources, 12, 18, 23–29, 45–47, 48–50
surveys, 34–35

T
tables, 35, 36, 52
thesis statement, 15, 21–22, 23, 36, 38
third person, 7
title page, 51–52
topic, 9, 15, 18, 19–21

V
validity, 34

W
Web sites, 24, 25–26, 27, 50, 55–56
works cited page, 18, 25, 28–29, 45, 48–50
writing process, 41–43